How Habits Influence Children,

… and Parents Too!

"Your beliefs become your thoughts
Your thoughts become your words
Your words become your actions
Your actions become your habits
Your habits become your values
Your values become your destiny"

Mahatma Gandhi

For all of you amazing parents,
To your greater life!

Routine Charts BONUS

As a way of saying thanks for your purchase and to guide you to get started, I am sharing a free kit to DIY routine visual charts.

http://www.zenpresspublishing.com/habit

Visit the link above to get access to them now.

In this bonus, you will get:

- A ready-to-print chart for a hassle-free morning routine for toddlers
- A ready-to-print chart for a quiet bedtime routine
- 2 templates to create your own routine charts (a simple chart and a racing game board chart)
- A selection of images to illustrate the routine steps

Table of Contents

Introduction 9

Chapter 1: Why habits though? 13

1.1 Anything can be mastered by habits 13

1.2 Human life is an accumulation of habits 15

1.3 The importance of forming habits in early childhood 16

1.4 It's ultimately the DNA of a family 18

Chapter 2: What habits can you bring? What is a routine? 21

2.1 The objective is to form character and emotional intelligence through positive habits 21

2.2 Positive habits can support discipline too 23

2.3 Routine grants a frame 25

Chapter 3: How 29

3.1 How to make a routine? 29

3.2 The key factors for a successful routine or habit 31

3.3 What to do if you need to break a bad habit 36

Chapter 4: Examples from the daily life with children..41

4.1 Lunch or dinner routines 41

4.2 Bedtime routine 42

4.3 The habit of a pause button and to breathe consciously
.... 44

4.4 The habit of sharing your story with your kids 47

4.5 The habit of avoiding the word no and the ritual of a monthly yes-day 48

Conclusion 51

Free routine templates 54

Also by the same author 56

Short biography 57

Introduction

Last weekend we had friends with three small children about the ages of our own visiting us. Needless to say, the house resonated with laughter and tears and transformed into a very animated place for the few days! Funny enough, many parts of the days ran much smoother than I would have expected, considering we were dealing with five little boys between one and six.

At meal times, everyone sang along and made their way to the dining room when we sang our little song "Heigh-Ho, Heigh-Ho, It's off to work we go" from *Snow White and the Seven Dwarves,* which for us is the signal to go wash our hands before eating. All of the kids participated in the toy cleaning race when I asked them to (here, also, we hum a short rhyme). And again at bedtime, even though the little guests did not want to stop their playing, they quickly joined our elephant patrol (yes, from *The Jungle Book*) when we moved to the bathroom to brush teeth.

My girlfriend was amazed and asked me: "How do you do that? They listen to you when you say something!" Well, I found it funny because I'm the first one to say that I wish my children would listen much more when I talk to them, but in that situation my answer was simple. "I don't talk to them, we sing." We sing a song for the different transitions in the day, and we have been doing this basically since they were born. It's our own secret funny family ritual and it almost always works to automatically get them on board with the day's schedule.

I used to think that self-discipline and planning hindered creativity, and I wanted to spend my day without schedules. To me, repetitive routines also sounded boring.

Well, I guess my children brought me back to reality. Try to explain to toddlers that you feel like staying longer on the beach and that they will just eat later. Actually, it might work right then because they only live in the present moment and enjoy playing in the sand. But you can be sure that it will all end up in tears later on because they will be extremely tired by the time you go home *and*, of course, completely starving. Also, there is no way you can catch up that extra hour you spent outside and still get them to bed at the usual time. They will need the same time to get ready, if not more because they probably respond badly to the stress of being pushed to hurry up (and don't forget—they're exhausted).

Yes, freedom and flexibility are always possible with small children, but there might be a high price to pay. Raising children can be draining and I got to a point where I needed more harmony and peaceful times in our home…

I started seeing routines as a way to keep my sanity on long days and as a way to be sure I wasn't just spending all my time taking care of the household, the basics, or discipline. I began putting routines into place that supported what was most important to me.

Best of all, routines have made it possible to start doing some of the things I always wanted to do with my kids, but never found the time for when I was bogged down with all that other stuff.

A good routine can really make that difference between a morning full of harmony and happiness and a morning with only tears or tensions. Also, especially at the end of the day, when we are all tired, a good bedtime routine allows opportunities for connection rather than screaming and using up all of our precious time together in discipline.

Habits brought by routines can be that strong. Of course it's nice to know these little tricks to handle daily challenges with small children. But I believe they are even more powerful for the long term.

It's a difficult world that we live in; our children should be prepared through strong values, and as parents we can benefit from developing a semi-automatic mode in our daily life to gloss over the basics and spend more time connecting and teaching precious life skills. And we can do this better when we are not overwhelmed by the daily, simple tasks of getting them cleaned, dressed, and fed. Even though I am a big fan of using these recurring moments to teach values and connect deeper, it's easier to tackle the big stuff when routines are in place and your day is more organized.

I want to bring a deeper message to parents through my books, as well as easy-to-use tips. As modern parents we are worrying about far more than just our kids sharing toys or fighting with their siblings. These are only occasions to help them grow stronger. Above anything, we want to develop our kids in a way that helps them to resist drugs and peer pressure or overcome fears developed from the modern-day horrors played out in the media. We want them to acquire qualities that matter related to character such as perseverance, curiosity, joy, gratitude, grit, forgiveness, how to deal with failure, how to manage adversity, how to form healthy relationships, and how to make sound decisions on their own.

Good habits brought by routines or rituals can greatly contribute to this over the long term. What we teach our children now will prepare the adult of tomorrow and remain with them for life.

Chapter 1: Why habits though?

1.1 Anything can be mastered by habits

Achievements based though repetitive tasks are just amazing. It's actually a rule of nature itself. How are river canyons created? Well, it's the regular water pressure of a river that cuts deep into a river bed. It then gets progressively larger year after year.

And the same applies to our human efforts to build skills over time.

I first want to give you some examples to illustrate the potential power of habits and routines on children.

Champions get to their maximum performance thanks to hours and hours of hard and regular training. If you think about it, the portion of talent is minimal in the overall equation of their success. It's really the muscle training and the discipline of integrating their reaction to certain situations until it is second nature to them that bring them to the top. They optimize their performance because they run on automatic mode. They spend days, weeks, or maybe months on improving one simple technique until the habit has stuck and turned into a natural ability. They master a focused approach to internalize perfection at high levels. They get there through regular hard work.

Intellectual competences follow the same pattern. I read a lot on raising bilingual children because of our own family situation. I am French, my husband is Italian, and we currently live in Germany; we were seeking some advice on how to integrate these cultural peculiarities in our family life so that the kids can benefit from learning three languages simultaneously. Research shows that a child can grow up completely bilingual (meaning that they can speak the two languages with the same ability and pronunciation as a native speaker) under the condition that between the ages of two and seven years old they are exposed regularly to the second language at least six hours a week (in about three sessions).

There are some other success factors, but the very basic requirement is "only" about two hours every other day roughly for their first six years! With this exposure, they have the ability to learn another language for life (of course, it'll have to be practiced further to stay). I find this so fascinating, considering how much I have battled to learn other foreign languages, and I will never reach the level of a native speaker, without even mentioning my very strong French accent….

One last example on the power of habits: if you are a musician, this will sound obvious to you. But, unfortunately, I am not, and it really amazes me to watch the progress of my little nephew playing the violin. We went on a family vacation together this Easter. I knew he had started to learn eight months ago, together with deciphering notes. But I remained speechless when he came to me with his song book, asked me to pick one song he would play for me, and started to play a very joyful piece of music.

To me, the violin is a very difficult instrument to play, and I'd thought a child would only be able to get some grinding noises (at best) after a few months. Well, the result of 20 minutes practicing every other day and one hour a week private lesson is mind-blowing. Imagine, within a few months you can start playing songs on an instrument, something you could not a year before!

1.2 Human life is an accumulation of habits

But habits don't come into play only for high performance or learning new skills. Most of our everyday behavior is also based on habit. It is quite shocking to realize that nearly all that you do each day is simply habit.

What did you do this morning when you woke up? Did you go straight to the shower or did you prepare your coffee? What do you tell your children when you separate for the day? What do you prefer to eat for lunch: a salad or a hamburger, if you have the choice?

As human beings, we are so habit driven. Think of how you react when you go on vacation in a foreign country. Sure, you can enjoy eating some new dishes. But how do you sleep in a bed that is not your own? Do you need some time to adjust when you arrive in an unknown place? If you practice yoga in your fitness club, do you have a favorite spot to unroll your mat or do you spontaneously change place every time you go and practice?

We would tend to think that most of what we do is the result of well-thought decisions, but it really is not. We subconsciously avoid change and have a certain fear of the unknown. It's in our human nature. Our comfort zone is what we know, and we just repeat it. Our daily life is an accumulation of habits most of the time. If isolated, each of these little habits doesn't really matter in itself. But what we cook every day, what we whisper to our child after the goodnight kiss, and how much physical exercise we get is extremely important over time—for our health, for our way of thinking, and generally for how happy we live our lives. We are creatures of habit, and so we should build positive routines in our lives. That's why habits are so powerful in shaping the characters of our children and regulating their days.

1.3 The importance of forming habits in early childhood

Children function much in the same way as we do, if not even more comforted by habits as their capacity for adapting to the unknown is far less developed. Because their experience of the world is much more limited, habits and routines are all they know and give them security.

Even babies inside the womb get accustomed to external noises and the voice of their mother. They can recognize a piece of music if it has been played regularly when they were still inside the belly, and experience shows the familiar sound will even quiet them after the birth when they hear it again.

Children get used to routines, and it shapes their expectations. It is a framework for the important moments of the day. Not only does this avoid lots of arguing, fighting, and endless negotiations, but routines are miraculous to fall back on when you're totally exhausted.

One day I was really sick with a nasty bug. It was amazing that I could still monitor my two children (two and five at that time) through their bedtime routine from my own bed. They would come to my bedroom and inform me each time they had progressed through the sequence. I think it was the smoothest evening ever!

Also, keep the ultimate benefits in mind (the big picture for your kids) through the management of everyday moments. Consider your home as the place where the consistent framework for your child's future will come from. It is the safe place that helps to shape values. Through a consistent and regular approach to daily life situations you can prepare, rehearse, and teach your child to handle a fast-paced, unknown world. It can be a great tool to support what you want to teach to your kids.

1.4 It's ultimately the DNA of a family

As parents, we often feel that time is flying and we don't have time for anything above the daily grind. At some point we all feel completely overwhelmed and are just navigating in survival mode between family and work. Routines and habits can really help if you feel stuck in a rut and if you are trying to move on to a greater life.

Life is too short for getting caught up in the basics and not having any energy left for the interesting stuff! As much as this may sound controversial, habits, and even repetitive routines, actually help to get away from the basic daily stuff that takes up too much of our time.

We have a limited capacity of energy to make decisions and go outside of our comfort zones. If all the basics occur in an automatic mode, then we free up some of our precious energy for more important decisions and more fulfilling activities. It's when we finally find some time to play with our children, spend some time together just doing nothing special, or organize an activity we always wanted to do but never found the time for it.

There's a famous saying from Zig Ziglar that goes, "If you aim at nothing, you will hit it every time." You can be sure to stay where you are if you have no concrete goals of changing. You need to aim at everything you are seeking to make it happen. And the same idea applies to parenting just as well. If you turn your priorities into clear goals, you will teach your children these precious life skills. Educating children is draining because we have to repeat the same things hundreds of times and go through similar situations over and over. But if we are consistent, the message will ultimately get through. It is hard work, and a clear vision will help you stay focused and determined to implement daily routines and supportive habits into your life. Educating our children is nothing else than another great project in our lives. Plan your course, review the goals regularly, and always work toward your destination. You can even create your own family statement to underwrite the adoption of worthy values and add even more focus to achieving them.

These habits, routines, or rituals we bring to our children's lives are what they will keep inside them forever. It will build their memories and shape their inner voice. They will remember the Saturday walks to the bakery to buy donuts and bagels for breakfast, the Sunday baseball games with Dad, or the traditional summer BBQ party as great family moments. If you demonstrate true empathy every time someone is hurt, even if it is during a simple siblings' fight, they will be inclined to feel the pain of others and develop a caring attitude at some point (though it might take years….).

The end result is the only thing that matters. Let's try to keep this in mind the next time we are in the middle of one of those chaotic days when everything goes wrong with the kids. How we react is what we are teaching them. So let's move on to the next chapters and see how we can unlock the power of routines and good habits in our children's lives to ease the days and teach strong values that prepare them well for life.

Chapter 2: What habits can you bring? What is a routine?

2.1 The objective is to form character and emotional intelligence through positive habits

As we saw before, habits are so present in our lives that we can cover many aspects of raising a child with their power.

They first can be a tremendous help in smoothing some typical parts of the day that are often difficult to manage with children, such as getting ready on time in the morning, eating what is on their plate, and behaving or going to bed in the evening without ruining everyone's night.

Also, children might not listen to what you say, but they will always repeat what you do. A routine that structures an activity is often welcomed by parents to help model how things should go. It's utterly important to model adequately what we want to teach, but it's sometimes difficult to do so because we ourselves have not mastered the skills we want to transmit. I don't want my kids to shout, but I often struggle at not yelling when things go awfully wrong. This is not the example I would like to set.... Routines help us to stay on track and have less of an opportunity for things to go wrong.

I suggest that you take some time to reflect on what you want to teach to your children.

This will help identify the areas where you need to work and focus on and help you state your clear objectives.

In my book Time Management for Parents, I teach how to create your own vision board to clarify what it is that you want to achieve in your life. It applies similarly when it comes to raising children. To help me manage our days, I have reflected on my vision of how I want my children to be as adults. I only imply character-wise, not the job I would expect them to do, where I would like them to live, etc. This vision gives me an overall direction on how I want to raise them. Let me share some of my educational priorities.

I value positive communication to teach compassion and negotiation, to express emotions, and assert their wants so that they build an enthusiastic and confident inner voice, believe in the abundance of possibility in this world, and take care of others.

I value a responsible you-don't-need-permission attitude because they should do things for themselves and not to please others. I also want to teach them that they can only influence the way they react to things because they can't control what others do.

I believe in the habit of repairing, be it a physical damage or reconnecting after breaks in communication, provided it comes from the heart. I think it's important to express a feeling such as, "What can I do for you, I did not like how this morning went..." because everyone should take ownership of their actions.

I want to teach that we work out problems together; we propose solutions and pick something viable for everyone, as a family.

2.2 Positive habits can support discipline too

I am not a fan of time-outs or punishment when children misbehave or show bad behavior; even though I really wish this would be the absolute and ultimate solution when they push my limits and I cannot think of anything else in the moment but to punish.

I am the first one to feel like yelling and isolate my son if he hits, claws his brother, or slams the door. But deep down, I know it will just make him even more upset and not help him to understand how he should react in a better, more socially-accepted way. I might put him in his room briefly so that he quiets down if nothing else works, but I usually accompany him to explain what went wrong and ask him what he thinks he could do to change the situation. I want him to reflect on his actions and to guide him to find an appropriate response.

I don't want him to be compliant but cooperative. I don't want to make him feel ashamed or shut down for a particular event, just because someone shouts louder. I don't want to force him to say sorry and let him believe this magically erases any attitude. I want him to feel true empathy for what happened and give him the opportunity to repair and improve the situation.

I think punishments with disconnected consequences like standing in a corner do not help with any of that. It's not going to teach how to manage frustrations and make amends with others. Of course, it's faster to count 1, 2, 3 and place them in a corner when they disobey, but the learning process is missing, and punishment without that teaching moment does nothing to help them prepare for the future.

I believe in the power of good habits over punishment for the long-term. As parents, we aren't really looking for only short-term obedience; we're also aiming to develop wonderful adults.

Positive habits can be precious tools when we discipline children, and if you can incorporate these habits into your parenting approach, you can only succeed in the big picture.

Consider the following habits and their implication for your child's future:

Validate feelings: it allows the child to be heard and to express their emotions in a healthy way. We all want to be understood and so do they. But it does not mean you accept it and bend to it as a parent. You just recognize the feeling and stand your ground. "I hear that you are very upset and you would like me to play with you, however I have to finish preparing dinner for now."

Encourage and guide problem solving: it sets the example and habit to look for a solution when something goes wrong rather than feeling upset, ranting, and positioning oneself as a victim. "What can we do so you can play and I can finish cooking? Would you like to bring a puzzle in the kitchen and I will help you while I cook?"

Allow the child to be part of the solution: it motivates them to be an actor in the process and to make decisions on their own. "Do you have any other suggestions?"

Repeat and show your unconditional love: it reassures them that they are not bad when they themselves cannot even understand their behaviors. It will make them feel that they can always come to you when something is difficult. It should always be clear to a child that your love doesn't enter into the balance when sanctioning a behavior. "I love you from the deep of my heart, but I really hate when you behave like this."

2.3 Routine grants a frame

A routine is a sequence of repetitive mini-habits around a specific activity in the day, such as getting ready in the morning or bedtime in the evening.

Children are children and as such do all sorts of things that we don't like, things that drive us nuts. The purpose of a routine is often to set our expectations and make it so easy and attractive to follow that they can't really deviate or get distracted by other (silly) ideas. The benefits of an established routine can be profound for your family. Here are the reasons why:

- It sets the rules and gives limits with love and firmness. Instead of barking instructions or constantly repeating that they cannot do this, they cannot do that, it allows you to assert positively what you consider important to respect in your home at certain times of the day.

- It creates a sense of belonging. It's the first step to establishing family rules. They get the clear message: "That's how we do things at home," or "We all do that in our family." You will be surprised to hear them teaching it to their little friends visiting your place.

- They know what to expect next. It's reassuring. It eliminates the unknown, the fear from the unexpected or the surprise of what comes next. It minimizes their need for adaptability. Children do live in the present moment much more than we do. That's why they can stay on an activity such as getting dressed forever. If it's fun, they get caught up in it. Time does not really mean anything to them, and they can be very reluctant to move on to something else in the middle of anything entertaining. But if they are reminded of what is happening afterwards, this raises their awareness of time passing and brings them a bit closer to our own expectations as a family.

- A routine acts as a third party. You are not the mean person to remind them of unpleasant things anymore. The rule or the sequence is hung on the wall. You can point to it when needed. Kids don't have to argue with you any longer.

- It provides a possibility to take ownership. Small children love to make their own decisions, and within the given framework they can decide about the how to execute. Think of a getting dressed routine. It can consist of the steps to take off the pajamas, put them under the pillow, put on a tee-shirt, and that they get the chance to pick out socks or a hair band that they like. This grants them a little responsibility in the process.

- It can be formulated at the level of understanding kids are capable of. Say you've depicted the routine with icons, images, or pictures—they can "read" it alone and can easily rephrase what they see. A picture is always worth a thousand words, even more for children.

Finally, it makes it easier for us to stay consistent. Parenting can be so draining... especially when you are tired. A routine helps to stay focused and to avoid the temptation to let it go for today.

Chapter 3: How

Maybe you're coming from a situation where you constantly feel overwhelmed, that your house looks like a tornado just came through and wiped all the shelves. Whatever you might say, the kids just continue doing whatever it is that you don't want them to and don't even seem to hear you. Or maybe you're just feeling clueless on how to handle their fighting and want to encourage them to be kinder to each other.

In any case, start thinking of the worst part of your day, what you aren't enjoying in your family life. That's where you urgently need to set up a routine first in order to shape things differently. Even if you only tackle a small portion of your day, start with that little timeframe. The big routines are built out of smaller ones. It'll come easier and easier to have a fulfilled and happy day when you master a few spots in your day. It's better to create a few smaller routines, practice, and build around them than try to completely organize your full day right from the beginning and feel frustrated at the difficulty.

3.1 How to make a routine?

Think of what you want to happen.

Keep it simple and cut it down to the bare minimum. Focus first on what would make the biggest difference time-wise and energy-wise, with what can motivate them to get there faster or help to prioritize difficult tasks first.

It will change over time anyway, don't worry. I have changed our morning routine already many times…

Last year I was lucky. They were so hungry in the morning that they would always rush to get dressed and get to their breakfast. I think getting dressed before breakfast is a good sequence anyway because they are basically ready to go at that point, and you could skip eating at home if pressed for time… This is what I mean by choosing ways to impact your time.

When we came to the point that breakfast was not a big enough motivation to get ready, I introduced the possibility of watching a five-minute cartoon if everybody is done (dressed and finished eating) by 8:00 AM. I cannot really remember a single day when we have not watched one!

Write it down and create a visual instruction.

You need to write it down for yourself as a cheat sheet for when things go wrong and you need to remember (in the middle of the chaos) what is supposed to happen next. It's your safe repository of the rule. Take the opportunity to do a creative activity around the new routine with your child. Explain what you are trying to put in place and make a visual chart together. Check out my free templates at the end of the book. Use images from toy catalogs or family pictures, stickers, and all sorts of material to create a cute board to hang where the routine will happen.

Try the new routine.

No need to say that it won't work the first time. Give it a try and expect the first days to go badly. But keep the focus, and after a week you will see some progress and where some steps might need to be adjusted. Only once it's working automatically (probably around four to six weeks), then you can add to your routine. I like to think of our routine as a sketch of how things should go in the big lines and that I fill out the details depending on the events and moods of the day.

Introduce the routine during a stable period (not during vacation or after a major event such as starting in a new school or the arrival of a little sister), ideally as early as possible from birth on and make it evolve over time coinciding with the needs of your family.

3.2 The key factors for a successful routine or habit

Have a visual or sensorial representation and playful elements in the routine.

After trying many different types of routine boards that we created ourselves, I can say that the ones that work best at our home are those with our own pictures depicted in the situation or funny cartoon characters cut out from magazines and when there is a gaming element into it.

Images, music, or signals are excellent triggers for young children. Always use images, don't write for children. For example, if you want your children to sort out their toys by themselves at the end of the day, then label the shelves or the containers with icons, not with words, so that they can easily associate what goes where with an image.

Our morning routine board is represented with a self-magnet (a funny picture of them on a kid's car) and each "task" is designed as a step on a race board (get up, potty, pajamas off, pajamas under pillow, getting dressed, choose socks, breakfast, shoes and jacket, cartoon) with two lanes for each of my children. Sometimes when they get stuck, I can even motivate them with the reward that the first one ready gets to choose the cartoon! There is also a clock drawn close to the arrival lane, and they know that they have to cross it before 8:00 AM.

You will always need to be a model.

Kids may not seem to listen to what you say, but they will always mimic what you are doing… or saying. We don't always realize it, but our modeling role as a parent is extremely important.

The best way to train your child to be polite is to put emphasis on your own good manners among adults. Don't expect them to say "thank you" if you don't usually practice with your partner, friends, or family! Even the youngest toddler can start learning the magic words, it's just another habit. Train your child to be polite, and the most efficient way to do so is to speak to them the way you want them to speak to you, too—polite, well-mannered, and pleasant.

Be consistent with regular practice.

Repetition, again and again, is how children learn. Staying consistently on course is what brings us to the target. A routine can only work if it is regularly used.

Give them ownership.

It's important to work together to establish the routine board. You can find some cute versions to buy on Etsy or TPT (Teachers Pay Teachers), but always try to customize it together. Your child gets a chance to participate in establishing the family rules and as such is more interested in following them. For a long time, I have had three participants to our morning routine because my older son decided his teddy bear also had to do it. That worked really well. The more they can decide within the framework, the better.

When we created the evening version, my children found it too boring, and I have added a two-minute sofa jumping exercise to get them to agree to the rest of the routine. I am still not sure I like this one (because it excites them rather than quieting them at the end of the day), but I have to say it is great fun and really efficient. They brush teeth and get into pajamas much faster and without complaining ever since we introduced that element. In the beginning, they wouldn't stop at two minutes, and it didn't help the evening routine at all. It got under control when we bought a timer that they set themselves.

The process of involvement is as important as the content, because without involvement, commitment will be missing for sure.

Make it easy so that it's impossible for them to deviate.

The routine won't do everything. It only sets the framework. It works just as anything else in life when it comes to achieving something new: you will never make any change if you don't create the small space for it. Always prepare the environment so that it is difficult for your child to deviate from the goals. Spend some time to remove distractions or temptations from the rooms beforehand. If you are trying to create a routine to get to bed earlier, then think of all the possible excuses that could come up and get in the way. Play? Clean the toys from the room. Potty? Have a toilet-stop step already included in the routine. Thirsty? Provide a cup of water on the nightstand.

Put the routine in place progressively over a long period of time.

Start with something small and make it evolve; don't get too detailed at first. Really make sure that you keep it simple in the beginning.

Also, if you want to develop some tools to help your child quiet down, be ready to introduce those tools and rehearse them first during calm times. You will only be able to resort to a calming song or a breathing technique during a tantrum or any overexcitement if your child has already associated it with a quiet state. Establishing that response could take many months.

Stay flexible during special circumstances.

Of course if your child gets sick or you are traveling, you can put a hold on some habits and rules. When traveling long journeys, the no-snacking habit should not apply. It would be inhuman to try to get toddlers to resist eating when everyone around them is doing so in the plane or in the car (which we all seem to do to help the time fly faster).

But once you have arrived at your destination, this is when you should return to the routine to unfold its reassuring character and cash in on the automatic mode. Even though you are not sleeping at home, the bedtime routine stays the same. This should give the children some structure in an unknown environment and help them understand that the evening follows the same logic even in another location.

Strengthen your vision and family mission statement.

Families who have clearly defined what they're aiming at and try to live their vision have it easier on a daily basis to stay consistent and motivated. Don't live day to day without a clear purpose in mind; don't let yourself get caught by the flow and apparent chaos of life. If you know what you want for yourself and your family, start to proactively assess your plan and share it with the other members of the family. This will start to put everything in motion toward achieving your goals.

Integrate some sort of reward at the end.

In his book The Power of Habits, Charles Duhigg conducted an impressive mass of research to understand how our habits shape us. He analyzed that habits always work best when following a pattern: a signal to trigger, an associated routine, a reward. With the reward not necessarily being the obvious benefit we get from the behavior. He often likes to give his own example of the bad habit he used to have of eating a chocolate chip cookie every afternoon. By learning how to analyze his habit, he figured out that the reason he walked to the cafeteria each day wasn't because he was craving a chocolate chip cookie. It was because he was craving socialization, the company of talking to his colleagues while munching. That was the habit's real reward.

But whatever the real benefit might be, it is a powerful motivation that drives the whole behavior and end result. Don't misunderstand me, I am not advocating to bribe children and to offer candies for whatever you want them to do. I strongly believe they should understand early enough that they do things for themselves and not to get something out of it, nor to please others. But offering stimulation, such as a little gamification or additional snuggling time, might be great motivation for toddlers to get through a routine. You might also want to spice it up with the right amount of responsibility as discussed earlier.

3.3 What to do if you need to break a bad habit

Sometimes habits go against what we actually would like. Over time a situation can develop and grow into a regular negative habit, and we might want to get rid of it. You may experience this with your child if you didn't put clear limits in place in the past and it has now come to the point that things have to change. The good news is that breaking bad habits works the same way as forming positive ones.

No big secret here. Cultivating new habits is often the best way to get rid of bad ones. The same always applies for any change, whether building up a new positive habit or reversing a negative one. Results will come easier and last longer if you give it time to stick. A radical change might work, but it might be difficult to enforce, causing lots of tears and arguing with children. Unless, of course, they have decided on their own to make the change (similar to when they decide that they do not need diapers any longer). When it comes from the child's decision, then our role is to make sure there is no temptation on the way that could cause a setback and to make everything easier for them to adjust to the new reality. If we are driving the change, a slow evolution and substitution is probably a better approach.

So, if you are trying to get your child to stop doing something, then I would suggest replacing the something with something else that he or she loves doing. If possible, identify what triggers the habit and what award the child gets out of it, and only replace the routine by an improved one. Do this for six to ten days in a row and the craving for the old activity or negative habit will be replaced by the craving for the newly introduced one.

A common request I often get from parents is tips to stop the pacifier. I like this example because the two approaches (radical or progressive) can work really well depending on the child. Here in Germany there is the legend of the pacifier fairy. Parents talk about it when the toddler gets older and the time has come to give up the beloved pacifier. They read a story about a fairy that helps small children to sooth themselves. One of her jobs is to distribute pacifiers to babies who need them.

Once a child feels ready, he can go to a special place in the woods and leave his pacifiers to the fairy, and she will give them to smaller babies who need them to fall asleep and calm down. Usually after a week or so of hearing this story, the child declares on his own that he wants to hand over his pacifiers and starts collecting them. Then the whole family goes for a walk to the "secret" place and ceremoniously deposits the pacifiers in the grass. You could organize someone to remove them so you can come back a few minutes later or the next day to acknowledge that they have disappeared. A little note or small present can also be found instead.

The other approach is to tell your child that he or she is now old enough and could be privileged to use a magical love bracelet. It's important not to propose it instead of, but to put the emphasis on the idea that this is something for older children. You can choose something else that you know will resonate more with your child, such as a stone or a key ring. Explain to them that every night before going to bed you will hold it close to your heart and charge the bracelet with all your love. Then during the day, when they might need some comfort and Mommy or Daddy are not there, they can hold it tight in their hand and feel the love flow that gives them strength.

At the beginning, pack the pacifier and the love bracelet together in their bag (with the pacifier maybe a bit less easy to grasp). It should not take long before they switch, especially if they are older and don't want other kids to make fun of them because they still use a pacifier. If the child does not transition naturally, then progressively limit the authorized use of the pacifier during certain times of the day (with full access to the love bracelet, of course) week after week. They will slowly forget about the pacifier and concentrate of the new tool!

On the contrary to introducing new habits, when breaking a bad one, you can take the opportunity to introduce the change during vacation or if you are traveling, as nothing is completely normal which makes it easier to switch habits in that case.

Chapter 4: Examples from the daily life with children

4.1 Lunch or dinner routines

Here is the example of our own lunch routine:

Give five-minute warning that lunch is almost ready.

Make and serve warm food for the kids (allow some time to cool down so that they don't complain or burn their tongues when they rush to eat).

Call the kids to the table.

Let them light a candle (that's the playful part to attract them and get them motivated to stop playing).

Sing a good appetite grateful song (to quiet down and teach long-term appreciation of what they have).

Eat and discuss all together.

Read a story while they're still eating.

I introduced the reading since it was taking ages for them to eat and because I used to rant that I had to wait for them to finish. Sometimes I would just start cleaning up and filling up the dishwasher. Even though I didn't feel that I was wasting my time by cleaning while waiting, I did not like it because we were missing an opportunity to connect. Very often they would finish eating by the time I was done with the household tasks so there was nothing left for them to do. I much prefer now that we have some nice time together. I am not impatient anymore for them to finish; I enjoy reading a story, and we all contribute to the cleaning together.

Lunch time used to be terrible. Kids were grumpy, loud, silly, goofy, and dirty. We could barely have a conversation, and they were not even eating well. Together with this routine and eating 30 minutes earlier (11:45 AM for lunch and 6:30 PM for dinner), it all changed dramatically.

You'd be surprised how a quiet and focused eating time can turn the fussiest kids into well-behaved and hungry children! As a result, the bad habit for a snack or bottle request (from my youngest one) totally disappeared.

4.2 Bedtime routine

The evening routine is one of the most important to me. For most parents, the morning routine is the most essential because you cannot afford to be late at the office or at school. Since it drives how you separate from your children, it may also influence your mood for the rest of the day. But I think the bedtime routine is even more crucial. In the same way, it does determine how we leave each other, here at the very end of the day. But what makes it trickier is that both parents and children are tired.

I hated it when the kids were so overexcited and would not listen to anything; it always ended up with us yelling to get them to quiet down and finally get them into bed much later than what we wanted. Most of the time, I felt our evenings were completely ruined. It was not fun to go through the battle of putting them to bed. I just prayed for this time of the day to be over as fast as possible. However I really wanted to relax, connect, and have some harmonious and snuggly time together. You know, something like holding their little hand while reading a story, having a big hug together, a few goodnight kisses, and after my child has smiled his last sleepy smile and answered me back, "I love you too, Mommy" to quietly close the door and sigh, full of happy thoughts and a filled heart.

Reality eventually got closer to this movie scene (after going through terrible battles for months and months) when I finally introduced a few working tricks.

For us, the key to a lovely evening has been relying a lot on the transition to the bathroom. Once they are motivated to move to the bathroom, the rest just follows quite smoothly…

Enter the elephants from The Jungle Book!

7:20 PM

Give ten-minute warning that playtime is ending, and they should start cleaning the toys.

7:30 PM

Set timer for two minutes of sofa jumping (only if toys are put away on time or else we move on when they are not cooperative).

7:35 PM

Preparation of the elephants for the evening patrol,

Transition to the bathroom while singing and miming the animals,

Teeth brushing and pajamas.

7:45 PM

Toilet, potty, or diaper change.

7:50 PM

Low light,

Story time (only if time left is permitting)

8:00 PM

Snuggling and quiet talk,

Prayer.

Of course, these are rough time indications and we don't look constantly at the clock. It takes us between 30 minutes and an hour to put them (happily!) to bed through this routine.

4.3 The habit of a pause button and to breathe consciously

I am a huge fan of slowing down and quiet times during the day. As an introvert, I recharge my battery by being alone and immersing in nature. I have learned how not to get dragged down by my own emotions while reconnecting regularly with my body. I believe this is a life skill very useful for children to acquire.

Learning to regularly listen carefully to your inner life teaches children, as well as parents, to become more aware of your own needs in a present moment, and therefore react more appropriately. It helps to understand that impulsive reactions are only happening in a short time span, and that they will go away with time anyhow. It teaches that unpleasant moments fly by just as anything else. It helps to accept the negative and be able to move on faster. It teaches not to hide anything as no state is permanent, meaning there is neither fear nor anger forever. Only how you react is what matters. And it's extremely important to accept and recognize emotions how they are, for what they are, or yourself just as you are. Life will always have a good deal of stress and situations we would like to be different. If you can teach your children to remain strong and happy under any circumstance and not waste time constantly trying to eliminate these, imagine what a gift this is for life! They will not be misled or defeated by their negative emotions. They will not overreact but be able to pause, reflect, and make wiser decisions. It really feels like being able to create a time distortion that enables you to live a given situation in slow motion so that you can understand it better. This is that powerful! Life becomes easier and more effortless.

To bring them to that, we regularly do breathing exercises. These sessions are some sort of mini-meditations for kids.

But we call them our froggy time, which sounds funnier to small children. Well, also we are French, so we have a certain affinity to frogs, I guess! But mainly because they love the animal and there is a famous book, Stay Still Like a Frog by Eline Snel. The only thing you see when a frog isn't moving in a puddle is its throat inflating and deflating as it breathes. You can show your child a video to watch a real frog in nature. They will visualize it better and know what you mean.

We sit in a circle on cushions and first hold each other's hands stating an appreciation, a purpose, or singing a small calming song. You can elaborate the routine over time, but in the beginning the only objective is to get them to pay attention to their breathing and what's happening in their body. You should first describe carefully how it feels to breathe in some fresh air through the nose holes, how it slowly goes through the lungs inside the chest and fills up the belly. Then describe how the belly deflates and the air we breathe out is warmer. Get them to put their hands on their tummy to better feel the movements. Observe the cycle while describing out loud what is happening. Through your words, they can experiment in their own body. We conclude how it feels good to do nothing, just listening to the inner life and letting the tensions go, all while our heartbeats are getting slower. At the end, I ring a little bell to indicate that the exercise is over, and we all go back quietly to our activity or play.

We do this almost every day. When we started we were doing it before lunch. Now we mainly practice when they get overexcited and need to cool down. We can do that because we have rehearsed weeks and weeks disconnected from the target of quieting down. Don't try to introduce this after a tantrum or a fight; it will never work in that situation.

4.4 The habit of sharing your story with your kids

When kids are younger, the idea of you being anything else other than a mom (or a dad) is hard to grasp for them. That's why I like to tell them every day one little thing I did and liked during that day, maybe one anecdote about something I did not like and how I handled it, and finally what I am grateful for and what I have learned. They get to know a bit of what I do as an author and a mompreneur. I really want them to understand what I do for a living. Also, I like to tell my sons stories of my own childhood when they are coming up with a similar situation I have encountered as a child. It's funny how fascinated they are by how we were as kids.

Both ways bring life lessons alive and more pertinent to them. It helps them to realize that I have been in their shoes; that I also struggle but then manage to overcome unpleasant daily situations. Besides this, it puts the habit in place that we do share stories and feelings on moments that we did not experience together. I believe it's important to keep them talking for when they will turn into teens. I want them to know that I am always here to listen to them, no matter what they have in their heart, and that I will not judge but listen and provide advice the best I can. I want them to experiment and practice regularly that our conversations are safe, respectful, and can help to analyze something difficult.

4.5 The habit of avoiding the word *no* and the ritual of a monthly yes-day

Did you know? A toddler hears the word no on average 150 times a day! How would you feel and react if someone was doing this to you all day long?

Cumulated over the first six years of their childhood, it amounts to hundreds of thousands of times when they are shown a negative vision to their surrounding world. As a consequence, we teach our children the world is a dangerous place, a place of restriction, limits and frustration, not really showing them an approach of abundance and creativity where they can thrive in self-confidence. If the day is full of no's, the child will tend to believe that the world is a negative place and that frustration is even normal.

As a parent, our job is for sure to try to anticipate all dangers, but we should refrain from expressing them out loud too often. Always silently scan for them, be ready to intervene if necessary, but keep the warnings for yourself if the danger is just a potential.

When the word no is used too frequently, toddlers just tend to tune it out after awhile. Also, the problem with saying no alone is that it does not help your son or daughter to learn what to do instead.

Try to use no only for emergencies, when there is an immediate danger. That way, your child will for sure stop and listen to you in the rare occasion when you really need to use the word. In the everyday situations, it's all about rephrasing it in a more positive way:

Describe what you see and how you interpret it. "You're throwing food. I understand that you are done eating."

Always give your child an idea of what they could do instead of focusing on what is not allowed. "You can say finished when you want to go and play."

Try to positively rephrase the message in a nicer way. "The food is for you to put in your mouth. I don't like when you throw it."

We probably all agree on this, but as parents we often have difficulties putting it into practice when it actually happens. In my case for sure, so I decided a couple of months ago to do a yes-day with my older son, just to put the emphasis on some positivity. The idea was to allow him to decide once a month how he wants to run his day and have him enjoy a frustration-free time. I was expecting that he would decide to wear shorts in the middle of winter, only eat chocolate and candies all day long, and request lots of expensive toys. I had actually prepared a few rules: nothing more than 20 miles away, nothing unhealthy or to the detriment of others, and we only spend 30 dollars max. I did not even have to take these rules out. Nothing that I dreaded actually happened. He chose not to go to daycare (well, obviously) and actually only asked for things we normally do but that he wanted to share exclusively with me. So we had a wonderful time at the swimming pool and at the playground, we went to eat a pizza in a restaurant and had one ice cream (yes, only one). He did not skip the nap. He just went a bit later than usual, and he asked that we snuggle and sleep together in my bed. In the end, the worst that he decided was to eat a few gummy bears and not brush his teeth before going to bed...

So nothing weird, not a single tear, nothing exaggerated, just spending time together in a purely harmonious way. What bliss! We have now done it three times and it only became more and more awesome to spend these moments bonding together. My girlfriends who tried it also reported similar experiences. This really made me think. Children only want to spend time and have fun with us. When we give them some dedicated attention and show our unconditional love, they behave much better and really thrive.

Conclusion

I am really fascinated by the amazing power of habits and how they can influence our lives, not only our children's lives but also our own.

I have experienced that it's much easier to enjoy our children and to be a happy family now that we have certain good habits in place. It's difficult enough to raise children since we are never sure that we are doing the right things. And parenting as a couple can sometimes make things even more challenging because we may have differing opinions from our partner. Families with strong routines and a clear goal translated through positive habits can definitely feel happier. Just to discuss the kind of home we all want in our family makes everyone more committed to achieving it on a daily basis. Keeping the end goal in mind helps everyone feel aligned with each other. As for any organization, it gives sense and a deep feeling of belonging when we all aim for the same goal. We speak more positively and we face challenges with more cheerfulness. We show much more understanding of each other's mistakes. We help each other and we definitely achieve more together.

Setting up routines and instilling positive habits has literally transformed my family life from a monotone day-to-day grind of parental caretaking to the more fulfilling joy of parental caregiving. Our family life now consists of richer emotions and stronger relationships. We all feel much more connected. It really shifted my perspective in life. True, I still do the same things, but I now see the deeper meaning in it and it's much more coordinated. Our days are by far smoother, we have more time for extras, I feel more consistent with my educational goals and my parenting project, AND I am much happier than ever.

I truly hope that you are now geared up with new tools and fresh ideas to handle challenging daily situations much more easily and, above all, to help you to stand up for your values and live them within your family. Live like highly effective people do, shape your own future by creating a mental vision and a strong purpose for your life and in general for any project, be it large or small, personal or for business. Break bad habits and turn them into positive ones. Make use of routines to free up some precious time for connecting and creating interesting times together.

Children grow very fast and we sometimes tend to forget it during the long days of these short years of their childhood. As parents we are growing the amazing adults of tomorrow. Each and every day we can contribute to shape their inner voice and what they will become by stacking up powerful habits in their mind.

I would love to hear about your experience. Also if you have any questions, please do not hesitate to reach out at anna.andersen@zenpresspublishing.com

I wish all the best to you and your family in this tremendously exciting endeavor of parenting. Happy family time!

And remember to sing, sing, and sing a lot to help get your message across!!!!

Your Own Routines

As a way of saying thanks for your purchase and to guide you to get started, I am sharing a free kit to DIY routine visual charts.

Visit the link below to get access to them now:

http://www.zenpresspublishing.com/habit

In this bonus, you will get:

- A ready-to-print chart for a hassle-free morning routine for toddlers
- A ready-to-print chart for a quiet bedtime routine
- 2 templates to create your own routine charts (a simple chart and a racing game board chart)
- A selection of images to illustrate the routine steps

Also by the same author

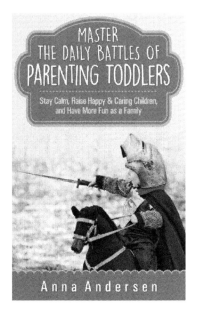 

Available in Kindle, print, and audio format

Short biography

Anna Andersen, author of the Zen Parent guides, is helping busy parents develop powerful habits to make family life with toddlers and preschoolers much easier.

She gives fresh suggestions on how to solve common challenges with small children and ultimately find simplicity, harmony, and happiness as a family.

As a mom of two, her books are always full of practical tips to react calmly and creatively to any situation and to raise self-sufficient, respectful, and happy children.

Anna is French and lives with her two young boys and her sewing machine in Munich, Germany.

Join the Zen Parents community on Facebook:

http://www.facebook.com/andersenanna

Disclaimer and Terms of Use: Effort has been made to ensure that the information in this book is accurate and complete, however, the author and the publisher do not warrant the accuracy of the information, text and graphics contained within the book due to the rapidly changing nature of science, research, known and unknown facts and internet. The author and the publisher do not hold any responsibility for errors, omissions or contrary interpretation of the subject matter herein. This book is presented solely for motivational and informational purposes only.

Limit of Liability and Disclaimer of Warranty: No book can replace the diagnostic expertise and medical advice from a competent medical professional. Please be certain to consult with your doctor before making any decisions that affect your health and the health of your children, in particular if you suffer from any medical condition or have any symptom that may require any medical treatment. The advice and strategies contained herein may not be suitable for every situation. Further, readers should be aware that internet web sites listed in this work may have changed or disappeared between when this work was written and when it is read, even though links are regularly checked.

Copyright: all rights Reserved. No part of this publication or the information in it may be quoted from or stored in a retrieval system or reproduced in any form or by any means such as printing, scanning, photocopying, electronically or otherwise without prior written permission of the copyright holder.

Published in Germany by ZenPress
© Agnes Famularo
Bothmerstr. 13
80 634 Munich

www.ZenPressPublishing.com

Thank you for your support of the Author's rights.

ISBN: 1518636659
ISBN 13: 978-1518636653

Made in the USA
Lexington, KY
09 May 2017